WITHOUT REGARD TO RACE

WITHOUT REGARD TO RACE

THE INTEGRATION OF THE U.S. MILITARY AFTER WORLD WAR II

BY HEDDA GARZA

A First Book
Franklin Watts
New York / Chicago / London / Toronto / Sydney

Cover art by Jane Sterrett

Photographs copyright ©: UPI/Bettmann: pp. 2, 11, 22, 25, 33, 36, 40, 48, 53; National Archives: pp. 8, 19; Library of Congress: pp. 9, 27; National Museum of American Jewish History, courtesy of the United States Holocaust Memorial Museum: p. 12; North Wind Picture Archives: p. 17; The Bettmann Archive: p. 20; Wide World Photos: pp. 28, 41, 43, 45; Archive Photos, N.Y.: p. 29; U.S. Navy Photo: p. 30; National Archives, Miles Educational Film Productions: pp. 32, 55; U.S. Army Signal Corps Photo: pp. 39, 50; U.S. Army Photo: p. 57.

Library of Congress Cataloging-in-Publication Data

Garza, Hedda.
    Without regard to race : the integration of the U.S. military
after World War II / by Hedda Garza.
        p. cm. — (A First book)
        Includes bibliographical references and index.
        Summary: Examines the racist attitudes that kept African-Americans from
meaningful service in the United States military and the changes that
occurred in the armed forces' policies during World War II.
        ISBN 0-531-20196-1
        1. United States—Armed Forces—Afro-Americans—History—Juvenile
literature. 2. World War, 1939–1945—Afro-Americans—Juvenile literature.
3. Racism—United States—History—20th century—Juvenile literature.
[1. United States—Armed Forces—Afro-Americans—History. 2. Racism.
3. World War, 1939–1945—Participation, Afro-American.] I. Title. II. Series.
UB418.A47G37 1995
355'.008996073—dc20   94-39898
                                                       CIP
                                                       AC

CONTENTS

1 ▼ SEPARATE ▼ AND ▼ UNEQUAL

On August 28, 1963, 300,000 people joined the March on Washington and heard Dr. Martin Luther King, Jr.'s stirring "I Have a Dream" speech. Very few of them realized that the civil rights revolution had started with another call for a March on Washington long ago. One person did.

He was A. Philip Randolph, one of the signers of the call for the 1963 demonstration. Twenty-three years earlier, Randolph had asked ten thousand black Americans to march on Washington to call for full equality in the armed forces and defense industries. That 1940 call was the groundbreaking opening shot in the fight for African-American equality.

By the time of King's speech, integration of the army, navy, Marine Corps and Air Corps had been accom-

A. Philip Randolph, leader in the World War II struggle for military integration, addressing a protest meeting

plished. The movement led by Dr. King focused on a much wider range of civil rights issues. In the South, a 1954 Supreme Court decision had outlawed school segregation, but black children still attended separate, mostly inferior schools. State laws called Black Codes or Jim Crow laws, passed after the Civil War, were still in effect. Signs reading "White Only" and "Colored" were posted in front of hotels, restaurants, playgrounds, swimming pools, public rest rooms, and water fountains. In most places, blacks were barred from voting.

Anyone who dared to complain was in grave danger. In the middle of the night, men wearing white sheets (members of the Ku Klux Klan) might come and burn fiery crosses in front of the homes of "offenders," drag them outside, and whip or even kill them.

In the rest of the nation long-standing racial prejudice, not laws, denied African-Americans the equal opportunity that was promised in the U.S. Constitution and in its amendments passed to end slavery and inequality. Most companies still hired black workers only as janitors and laborers.

During the Great Depression years of the 1930s, mil-

**Young boy at a segregated water
fountain in the South in 1938**

lions of Americans, of every race and ethnic group, lost
their jobs and watched helplessly while their furniture and
clothing were tossed out onto the streets because they
could not pay their rent. About 13 million African-Americans, the largest racial minority in the United States, suf-

fered more than any other group. Because of racial prejudice, they were the last hired and first fired.

The president of the United States, Franklin D. Roosevelt, had pushed his New Deal programs through the U.S. Congress, putting many people back to work in government projects such as building roads, bridges, and dams. Despite this, there still weren't enough jobs to go around until threatened involvement of the United States in a worldwide war made it necessary to reopen factories to produce tanks, guns, ammunition, and other military supplies.

The threat came from Germany, where a dangerous dictator named Adolf Hitler and his followers in the Nazi party had risen to power. Like the Ku Klux Klan, they believed in the racial superiority of "Aryan" people—white Christians. The Nazis labeled everyone else "inferiors" and planned to rid the world of them.

Hitler's powerful army swept into Austria and Czechoslovakia. "Today Germany, tomorrow the world!", Hitler bellowed at cheering crowds. Anyone who dared to oppose the Nazis was jailed or murdered. In Europe, there were very few blacks. Jewish people were the largest minority. Nazis rampaged through Jewish neighborhoods, beating up people and smashing shop windows. Jewish

A group of evicted sharecroppers camping along the highway in Missouri during the Depression. They had demanded their legal share of government payments to growers.

**Polish Jews being loaded on trains
headed for an extermination camp at Chelmno**

children were thrown out of their schools and assaulted by other children who had joined the Nazi Hitler Youth. Finally, Jews were rounded up and shipped off by the trainload to prisons called concentration camps. Before the war ended, at least six million Jewish people were exterminated in gas chambers in what the Nazis called the "Final Solution" to the Jewish question and what the world later called "the Holocaust." Hardly any Jews at all were left alive in Europe.

The dictator of Italy, Benito Mussolini, and the militaristic leaders of Japan gradually joined forces with Nazi Germany. They tested their latest military equipment and air forces in "little wars"—the Italians massacring thousands in the African nation of Ethiopia; the Japanese doing the same to people in China; and Hitler and Mussolini together helping another dictator, Francisco Franco, topple the democratic government of Spain in a bloody war.

The governments of Great Britain, France, the United States, and the Soviet Union (now Russia) made pacts with the three aggressors, hoping they could avoid another world war. It had been only twenty years since the First World War had cost hundreds of thousands of lives.

In September 1939, Hitler broke all his agreements. Powerful Nazi armies swept into Poland, then quickly grabbed Denmark, Norway, Holland, and Belgium, and surrounded France. England and France were forced to declare war against Germany. German rockets and bombs rained destruction on London. At the end of June,

Nazi armies poured into the Soviet Union. Almost all of Europe was at war.

President Roosevelt realized that a victory for Hitler's forces could mean the end of democracy everywhere. The United States sent supplies to England and prepared to join the conflict. Thousands of factories reopened to produce armaments.

Americans were urged to enlist in the armed forces, but black men were not included in that call. The air corps and marines barred them completely. The navy allowed them to join only as messmen (kitchen staff and cleaning men). The army had maintained a few all-black units, but, together with the navy, told potential black recruits there were no openings.

African-Americans believed that men who showed their bravery in battle had a better chance of being treated as equals when the war was over. Nazi propaganda often ridiculed the American democracy for its own unfair treatment of minorities. Black Americans hoped that now an embarrassed government would end racial segregation in the armed forces.

All during World War II, African-Americans and their supporters waged a battle against two enemies—the Axis powers of Germany, Italy, and Japan, and discrimination and segregation within the U.S. military forces that were trying to save democracy.

2 ▼▼ A LOSING BATTLE

Since the days of the American Revolution, black Americans were permitted to bear arms only when there was a serious emergency. In peacetime, their contributions were quickly forgotten.

During the American War of Independence against Great Britain, about five thousand black men fought side by side with thirty thousand white colonists in George Washington's Continental Army. They froze together at Valley Forge and celebrated victories from Bunker Hill to Yorktown.

Soon after independence was won, laws were passed that barred black men and American Indians from the state militias, later to become the U.S. Army. Slavery was permitted to continue. It expanded like a hideous mushroom in the South.

The army turned away African-American volunteers

during the War of 1812, when Great Britain again attempted to assert its power. In Louisiana, desperate commanders, short of troops, allowed a separate corps of black militiamen to fight in the key Battle of New Orleans. The newly formed U.S. Navy also banned black sailors, but when it ran short of crews to fight the powerful British Navy, it recruited black men. White and black seamen shared sleeping quarters, worked, ate, fought, and died together. The navy remained integrated for several years, but the army continued to ban African-Americans. The black men who had battled and died at New Orleans were conveniently forgotten.

During the Civil War, black people, slave and free, hoped that a Union victory against the South's Confederacy would mean an end to slavery. Runaway slaves, however, who arrived at Union Army camps were seized and returned to their masters. President Abraham Lincoln feared that if he allowed them to fight, the slaveholding border states would join the Confederacy.

Prominent abolitionists (anti-slavery blacks and whites) prodded the president to act. When several battles were lost by the Union Army, Lincoln issued the Emancipation Proclamation, freeing the slaves. Then a call went out for black volunteers. Before the end of 1863, about one hundred thousand former slaves were in separate divisions of the Union Army, led by white officers.

At the end of the Civil War, twenty black servicemen were decorated for bravery. Four all-black army units were established and stationed in the West at isolated army posts to fight American Indians struggling to keep their land.

Lithograph of the Battle of New Orleans, where General Andrew Jackson brought in a corps of black militiamen to fight alongside white soldiers

The Indians called them "Buffalo Soldiers," perhaps because of the color of their skin. If any of the black soldiers felt uncomfortable about fighting other nonwhites, little was said. They proudly wore the uniform of a government that promised them full citizenship.

At first it seemed those promises would be kept. Congress passed laws and amendments to the Constitution guaranteeing the newly freed slaves their rights. Federal troops protected them in the South. The Freedmen's Bureau was established to educate, feed, and help former slaves build new lives. "Reconstruction" programs offered blacks hope.

But in a few years, the economy went into a severe depression. The halls of Congress resounded with arguments over the cost of "Reconstruction." In 1872, the doors of the Freedmen's Bureau slammed shut. Four years later, federal troops were withdrawn from the South. Many ex-Confederates took revenge for their defeat. The Black Codes were passed. Rifle clubs and the Ku Klux Klan launched a reign of terror to enforce the separation of the races.

The government and many people in the North ignored the crimes in the South and concentrated on industrial growth and expansion West and overseas. The Buffalo Soldiers and sixteen volunteer African-American regiments fought in the Spanish-American–Cuban War in 1898. The victory gave the United States not only the colonies of Puerto Rico, Guam, and the Philippines but also a great influence over Cuba. Yet there was little recognition for black fighters, and they were often the objects of ridicule and abuse.

A shameful episode took place in Brownsville, Texas, in 1906. One hot night, gunshots rang out in a white area near the army camp there, leaving one dead and two injured. Three companies of 167 men of the African-American 24th Division were blamed, insulted, and at-

All-black cavalry unit of "Buffalo Soldiers" sent to the West at the end of the Civil War to maintain peace between white settlers and American Indians

tacked by white townspeople. A local grand jury found no evidence that any of the black soldiers were involved, but the army ordered the dishonorable discharge of *all three companies!* On April 28, 1972, sixty-three years later, the

African-American troops of the 9th Cavalry Regiment charging up San Juan Hill in Cuba during the Spanish-American War in 1898

secretary of army cleared the black soldiers. Only one eighty-six-year-old veteran was still alive to receive his honorable discharge.

By 1915, World War I was raging in Europe. Although the United States did not enter the war until April 1917, Congress immediately passed the Selective Service Act, requiring all males between the ages of twenty and thirty to register for military service. Blacks were recruited into existing segregated units.

The slogan of World War I was "Make the world safe for democracy," but there was little democracy at home for blacks. In many places where black troops were stationed, whites rioted against them. W.E.B. DuBois, a much respected leader of the National Association for the Advancement of Colored People (NAACP), urged black Americans to postpone their struggle for equality until after the war.

Only forty thousand out of three hundred and fifty thousand black draftees were sent into action. The segregated 92nd Infantry Division served with the American forces, and four regiments of the 93rd Infantry Division fought alongside the French Army.

American military authorities advised French commanders to keep their troops away from the black soldiers and not praise them much. Racists were concerned that the French would "ruin" black men by treating them as equals. Despite this advice, the French troops showed respect for the "Buffalos," as they were still called, and honored three black American heroes with France's highest military honor, the Croix de Guerre.

During World War I, the African-American 93rd Infantry Division from New York fought alongside the French Army. Here, in 1918, officers of the division pose with a French child.

In contrast, the black Americans of the 92nd Infantry were poorly treated. They received very little training, and many of their southern white officers insulted them and reported unfavorably on their achievements.

When the war ended in 1918, black soldiers returned to lynchings and race riots in several cities. Many were still wearing the uniform of the army that had made the world "safe for democracy" when they were attacked. An angry W.E.B. DuBois of the NAACP now advised all those who opposed racial inequality to fight a "more unbending battle against the forces of hell in our land."

War Department officials met to hear testimony and make a decision on the future role of black men in the military. A white officer of the 92nd Division told the army committee that racism was so strong it was "difficult to obtain a true appreciation of the worth of the colored man as a soldier." His was one friendly voice against a chorus of criticism. For instance, another officer called Negro combat soldiers "naturally cowardly."

Black veterans were furious, and the NAACP called for a congressional investigation, but they were ignored. In 1922 and again in 1939 on the eve of World War II, the War Department announced that segregation would continue. Even in an emergency situation such as the war against Hitler, only 10 percent of the U.S. Army would be composed of segregated units for black Americans. The navy, air force, and Marine Corps would continue to select their own volunteers.

With the racist forces of Hitler's Nazis swallowing up the world, the war for equality at home had entered a new phase.

3 VV VOLUNTEERS WANTED: NO BLACKS NEED APPLY

In 1939, President Roosevelt, advised by the War Department that preparations for national defense would be threatened if segregation was ended, signed a new Selective Service Act that ordered segregation's continuation.

To organize resistance to racial discrimination in the armed forces, black leaders formed the Committee for the Participation of Negroes in the National Defense. The marines, air force, and navy were all begging for volunteers. Black Americans and their friends pressured these branches to open their doors to black men. The navy finally agreed to accept a few African-Americans, but only as messmen, purportedly "in the best interests of general ship efficiency."

To quiet the storm of protest, Congress authorized the

After many protests by African-Americans and their allies in 1941, a group of black men are permitted to enlist in the Army Air Corps for assignment to a segregated squadron.

use of civilian aviation schools for the training of black military pilots. When their training was completed, however, they were told that they could not join the air force because there were no black units! A black newspaper printed a photograph of airplanes on a factory assembly line. The caption read, "Warplanes—Negro Americans may not build them, repair them, or fly them, but they must help pay for them."

Presidential elections were scheduled for the fall of 1940. Troubled by increasing opposition, two months before election day, President Roosevelt ordered the War Department to issue a statement that of the first 400,000 men drafted, close to 10 percent would be black men. Black air units would be organized and "colored men will have equal opportunity with white men in all departments of the Army," the president promised. In January 1941, a segregated base for an African-American air corps unit was constructed in Washington, D.C., at the cost of millions of dollars. It was located only 40 miles (64 km) away from Maxwell Field, an all-white base with miles of unused space.

To black Americans it sounded like World War I all over again. A week before election day, black leaders including Walter White, executive secretary of the NAACP, Lester Granger of the National Urban League, and A. Philip Randolph, president of the all-black union the Brotherhood of Sleeping Car Porters, met with the military chiefs and President Roosevelt.

The black spokesmen suggested steps toward integration of the military and the selection of officer candidates without "regard to race." Army heads immediately turned down their proposals, claiming that even gradual changes would harm morale.

To sweeten the bitter pill, a week before the election, one black colonel, Benjamin O. Davis, was promoted to the rank of general, the first black man to hold that rank. William H. Hastie, a black Harvard Law School graduate, was named civilian aide to Secretary of War Henry L. Stimson.

It was not enough. This time black Americans refused to drop their demands for equality at home. They said that they wanted to fight against Hitler's Nazi forces in Europe and also against "the Hitlers in America." President Roosevelt listened more closely, however, to the

Walter White, executive secretary of the NAACP, a prominent leader of the struggle for integration of the U.S. armed forces during World War II

advice of War Secretary Henry Stimson, who frequently mentioned that his ancestors had been abolitionists. All of his decisions against integration he claimed, were based on the need for military efficiency.

Years later, when Stimson's diaries were published, his real feelings were exposed. On September 30, 1940,

Lester B. Granger receiving the Presidential Medal for Merit from Secretary of the Navy James Forrestal for his assistance in integrating the Navy during World War II

for example, he had characterized the possibility of black men being admitted to the air force as "a disaster." He joined the chorus of southern racists who insisted that black leaders pressing for military integration were actually looking for "social equality," and he even raised "the impossibility of race mixture by marriage."

A. Philip Randolph and other black leaders grew tired of useless meetings with government officials. Believing that only a mass protest march would have an impact, they sent out a call for ten thousand black Americans to participate in a March on Washington on July 1, 1940. As news of another insult, this time about the donation of blood, spread, interest in the march escalated.

When injuries in the London bombings mounted, the American Red Cross launched a national drive for blood donors. Dr. Charles Drew, the black scientist who had discovered a method for preserving blood for transfusion, was asked to head up the program. When he learned that blood plasma would be collected and separated according to race, he resigned. Dr. Drew knew better than anyone that there were no racial differences in human blood.

Pressured from all sides to call off the march while the president studied the matter, Randolph refused. He knew that the president had the power as commander in chief to issue a mandatory rule, called an executive order, to end discrimination in war plants with defense contracts and in the armed services.

Less than a week before the scheduled march, predictions were that at least fifty thousand marchers would come to Washington on July 1. President Roosevelt issued Executive Order 8802.

Henry L. Stimson, secretary of war during World War II. Stimson insisted on continued segregation of the armed forces.

Burning ships at the U.S. naval base at
Pearl Harbor after the surprise Japanese
bombing raid on December 7, 1941

Military integration was not mentioned in the order, although the president emphasized equality of treatment. Discrimination in defense plants with government contracts and in the hiring of government workers was prohibited. A Fair Employment Practices Committee (FEPC) was established to enforce the ruling. Black Americans needed jobs. The march was called off.

By September 1941, almost twenty-eight thousand African-American men had been drafted, most of them assigned to service groups, to be used as ditchdiggers and truck drivers throughout the war. Although some defense plants hired black workers, many continued to discriminate. The FEPC had only limited enforcement powers.

On December 7, 1941, Japanese bombers in a surprise raid rained destruction on a large part of the American naval fleet stationed in the Pacific at Pearl Harbor, Hawaii. Deep in the bottom of one of the ships, performing his messman chores, a black sailor named Dorie Miller heard the explosions and raced to the top deck. With almost no weapons training, he grabbed one of the big guns and, with bombs exploding all around him, he shot down three of the Japanese bombers. Dorie Miller received the Navy Cross for bravery, but he remained assigned to mess duty.

President Franklin D. Roosevelt's voice that day was heard over millions of radios officially declaring war on the Axis powers.

The army, still unable to build enough segregated training facilities for black recruits, urged the other

William Hastie, civilian aide to Stimson, who pressed for the use of black soldiers in combat

branches to take black volunteers to fulfill the promised 10 percent quota. Blacks were enraged when they learned that a committee appointed by Secretary of the Navy Frank Knox to "study" the question insisted that the "characteristics" of blacks made them fit only for messman's duty. Knox suggested that the marines would find it easier to segregate black recruits.

President Roosevelt urged Knox to "invent something that colored enlistees could do in addition to the rating of messman." In April 1942, Knox reluctantly announced that the navy would permit fourteen thousand black men to enlist for general service. The Marine Corps, part of the navy, started training its first all-black battalion that summer—and it was a labor battalion, not a combat one. There were no training programs for black officers.

Stimson's determined civilian aide William Hastie refused to ease up the pressure on his "unprejudiced" boss. In early 1942, he pointed out that the promise to assign black soldiers to combat units in the same ratio as whites had been broken. The vast majority of black soldiers, regardless of their educational levels, were assigned to so-called service

Skilled African-American worker in a war plant during World War II. President Roosevelt intervened to ensure the hiring of all workers regardless of race.

units. They worked as laborers, not soldiers. They belonged to water supply, ammunition, and gasoline supply battalions. In the countryside they fought fires and landscaped bases. In cities they acted as moving men. In the air corps they worked as cleaning teams in "aviation squadrons."

The NAACP proposed the formation of a volunteer integrated combat division. The War Department turned down the suggestion, claiming that army officers refused to use black soldiers in combat. Actually, a planning group of the Army General Staff had already made a similar suggestion.

Instead, the War Department created four new black infantry divisions, each one with fifteen thousand men, and announced they would soon be active. "Soon" turned out to be a long time off.

All during 1942, Americans anxiously followed the progress of the war. It was not going well. The Japanese had defeated most of the American forces in the Pacific. The Nazis had swallowed up a huge chunk of territory in the Soviet Union. Allied troops were bogged down battling the Nazis in North Africa. The all-black 2nd Cavalry Division was there, demanding to join the fighting. NAACP leader Walter White visited them and reported back that he had never seen "more depressed troops." Even Secretary of War Stimson described the problem as "very explosive and serious."

4 DOUBLE V

The vast majority of African-American troops were left in the United States, most of them stationed at training camps in the South. Their segregated recreational and living quarters were usually substandard. Even worse, when on leave in nearby communities they were frequently insulted, beaten, and even hanged or shot.

Before Pearl Harbor, in a wooded area at Fort Benning, Georgia, Pvt. Felix Hall was found hanging from a tree with his hands tied behind his back. Army authorities were ridiculed when they called Hall a suicide and never found the criminals.

At Fort Sill, Oklahoma, a young black soldier wrote a letter to his family telling them he would "just as soon fight here for our rights as to do it on some foreign battlefield."

**Officer dedicates first pilot training
school for officers of the all-black 99th
Pursuit Squadron of the U.S. Air Corps.**

Black soldiers deeply resented the better treatment sometimes given to German and Italian prisoners of war. In many of the restaurants in the South at which black soldiers were not permitted to eat, German and Italian prisoners laughed and drank with their guards. And so few African-Americans were elected for officer training that it became inefficient to create segregated facilities. At Camp Wheeler, Georgia, the only black officer candidate lived alone in a two-story apartment and ate by himself.

By the end of 1942, except in the Air Corps, officer candidate schools were integrated. White and black soldiers studied together and shared the same barracks and mess halls. Relations between the men improved enormously. There was almost no publicity about this successful experiment in integration.

Once African-American officers graduated, however, they were always placed under the command of white officers in charge of black troops. Some of the white officers regarded their assignments as punishment and were openly racist. The commander of a black unit in Pennsylvania, for example, prohibited his troops from associating in any way with white women. It would be "considered rape," he announced, and added that the penalty would be death!

As pressure increased to send black men into action, a number of service units were sent to Great Britain, awaiting orders to move on to combat areas. Most British citizens treated the black soldiers as equals. Some Americans tried to tell the British that blacks had tails and were dangerous. British officers told their soldiers not to argue with Americans over racial issues.

Trying to avoid violence, Gen. Dwight D. Eisenhower, commander in chief of the European Theater of War, issued orders forbidding the "spreading of derogatory statements" about black troops. In 1943, a photograph in *Life* magazine of black soldiers dancing with white English girls in a London nightclub caused an uproar. Threatened by a boycott by American white soldiers, some public places in Great Britain barred blacks. Nevertheless, when Walter White toured England in 1944, he said many American black GIs had their "first experience in being treated as normal human beings and friends by white people."

In January 1943, the air force announced that it would open a segregated officers candidate school for black airmen, despite the fact that other branches of the armed services had by then integrated such facilities. An air force commander commented that the all-black 99th Pursuit Squadron had no reason for existence except to provide a separate place for African-Americans. William Hastie resigned his post in disgust.

A wave of protest forced the air force to reverse its decision on the school and to send the 99th Pursuit Squadron to North Africa, under the command of Col. Benjamin O. Davis, Jr., General Davis's son. There, the

Gen. Dwight D. Eisenhower addressing paratroopers preparing for the D-Day invasion of Europe during World War II

Sixteen members of the first
all-black Army Air Force combat
unit, the 99th Pursuit Squadron

Lt. Col. Benjamin Davis, Jr., the highest-ranking
African-American officer in the Army Air Force,
giving some final pointers to a trainee

commander of the Fifth Air Force kept them sitting around for many months, out of the action.

During the hot summer of 1943, race riots broke out in several cities. The worst one took place on June 20 in Detroit, Michigan. Twenty-five African-Americans and nine whites were killed, and the governor had to call in federal troops to calm things down. When a newspaper photo showed a police officer holding an injured black by both arms while a white policeman struck him in the face, anger swept black communities across the nation.

A large letter *V* for victory had become a favorite wartime symbol. Now a Double *V* became the symbol of black America. One *V* stood for victory over the Axis powers; the other for victory over racism at home.

In January 1944, Secretary of War Stimson lit a larger flame under the already boiling pot when he announced that the all-black 2nd Cavalry Division, waiting to join the fight in North Africa, would be officially called a "service unit"—that is, not allowed to enter combat. Stimson claimed black men were "unable to master efficiently the techniques of modern weapons."

To try to quiet the uproar, the navy finally accepted its first black officers, and the War Department ordered that recreational facilities at army bases would be shared by

One of the newspaper photos of the 1943 Detroit race riot that stirred up anger in the black community. A police officer holds a black man's arms while another policeman strikes him.

42

all servicemen. Many commanders continued segregation by scheduling different times of use for blacks and whites. Pamphlets and a film praising black soldiers were released. Most black Americans were not impressed. They knew that blacks were still waiting to join the fight.

Once again a new presidential election was about to take place, causing a flurry of action in the White House. President Roosevelt asked the Coast Guard, Marine Corps, and the navy to take more black recruits. The black 92nd Division was shipped off to Italy, and a few units of the 93rd were sent to the Pacific.

In early 1944, Secretary of the Navy Knox died, and James Forrestal took over his post. He appointed Lester Granger, black former secretary of the National Urban League, as his aide. Most African-American sailors were still working in ship kitchens or laboring on docks. In a short time, two all-black antisubmarine vessels were sent to sea and the crews of twenty-five ships were integrated without any problems erupting.

Forrestal and Granger had just started to make a dent in navy segregation when a tragedy occurred. On July 17, 1944, at Port Chicago in San Francisco Bay, black service units had been assigned the dangerous work of loading

Seabees repairing damage at Port Chicago in San Francisco Bay after July 17, 1944, explosion killed 250 black sailors and nine white naval officers

ammunition ships. A giant explosion on the docks left three hundred men dead and even more injured. Among the dead were 250 blacks and their 9 white officers.

A few weeks later, survivors of the tragedy were told to unload other ammunition ships. More than half the men were too terrified to even begin the work. A few dozen men continued to refuse and were charged with mutiny: they were given long prison sentences and dishonorably discharged. After the war, these men were restored to active duty.

In July 1945, on the Pacific island of Guam, white marines and black navy men clashed over the right to date local women. After rioting between the two groups, forty-five black navy men, but no marines, were convicted and given long sentences. Once again, they were cleared after the war, when the Marine Corps admitted that white marines had been the main troublemakers.

Sixty-nine percent of the truck drivers in the European Theater of Operations were black. They hauled tons of materials from ports to the advancing armies. They stayed at the wheel without sleep for thirty-six-hour shifts, with land mines exploding under them and bombers raining death on them. They received no medals.

Black soldiers and sailors in service units knew their work was important. Soldiers could not fight without ammunition and supplies, without men rebuilding bombed-out bridges. But they also knew that many Americans believed that only white men were capable of actual fighting. By early 1944, some 134,000 black troops were still waiting out the war in England.

5 IN THE LINE OF FIRE

As in all other wars since the American Revolution, a small number of black men were finally permitted to fight when the military situation grew desperate.

In the skies over Italy, the men of the 99th Pursuit Squadron, calling themselves the "Lonely Eagles," were sent into combat. They shot down several German planes and proved that black men could serve valiantly in the air force.

After months of stalling and insults, the 92nd Infantry Division, still called the Buffalo Soldiers, fought alongside the Fifth Army and won many medals in six months of heavy battle. Gen. Mark Clark, commander of the Fifth, later said, "They were glorious."

Military strategists had come up with a bold plan to

catch Nazi forces in a two-way squeeze between American and British armies coming in from the coast of France and the Soviet Red Army pushing in from the east. On June 6, 1944, this long-awaited "second front" opened when 185,000 Allied troops landed on the beaches of Normandy, France. Five hundred African-Americans of the 320th Barrage Balloon Battalion were with them, launching huge balloons over the heads of the landing forces to hide them from German bombers.

Three days later, about seven hundred African-American tank fighters of the 762nd Division were shipped across the Atlantic. Segregated from white troops, they stayed in the bottom of the ships for the three-week-long journey. Some of them said they could imagine how black Africans felt on seventeenth-century slave ships.

They were the first all-black tank battalion in history, and they intended to prove their worth. Fighting their way across Europe, they rode over land mines and booby traps, protecting the white infantry units marching behind them.

In mid-December they rolled toward Belgium, where a terrible battle was in progress. The Germans had broken through Allied lines. The Battle of the Bulge had started, Germany's last desperate offensive. The 762nd

African-American naval mess attendant Dorie Miller receiving medal for his heroism at Pearl Harbor in 1941

Gen. Dwight D. Eisenhower touring the Sicilian front with President Franklin D. Roosevelt on December 8, 1943

won a victory in 4-foot (1.3-m) deep snow as they broke through to join the battle, proving beyond a doubt that they were fighting men. Except in the black-owned press, their contributions were seldom publicized.

As the war raged on, replacements were desperately needed for those who had died or were wounded or captured. General Eisenhower called on black troops to volunteer as infantry replacements. When more than five thousand African-American men in service units volunteered, Eisenhower revised his plan, accepted twenty-five hundred, and assigned them to small, segregated units.

During these actual final battles, of course, white and black soldiers found themselves fighting and dying together. Before that happened, the majority of the white soldiers had said they agreed with army segregation. Later polls showed that three-quarters of the men had changed their minds. Gen. Benjamin O. Davis wanted this fact publicized. Instead, as soon as the war in Europe ended, the black platoons were sent back to their service units. Their record, as well as the heroism of the segregated tankers and "Lonely Eagles," was conveniently forgotten. President Roosevelt died on April 12, 1945, knowing that victory was close at hand. Germany surrendered on May 7. Hitler committed suicide in an underground bunker as Russian troops closed in. During August—after the new president, Harry S. Truman, ordered the atomic bombing of two Japanese cities, Hiroshima and Nagasaki—Japan, also surrendered.

6 VV BITTER FRUITS OF VICTORY

African-American veterans left the still-segregated military and returned home determined to win full equality in all of society, starting with the right to vote. White southern racists were just as determined to have things the way they were before the war. The two forces were bound to clash.

Senator Theodore Bilbo of Mississippi said that "red blooded Anglo-Saxon men should stop Negroes from attempting to vote by any means." An American Legion post commander wrote to General Eisenhower that he had seen "pictures of black soldiers dancing with German girls." He warned that "if they expect to return to the South, they are very likely on their way to be hanged or to be burned alive at public lynchings."

These were not just empty threats. The number of attacks against black people increased dramatically. In

Senator Theodore Bilbo of Mississippi during a Democratic party primary in 1946. Bilbo said that African-Americans should be banned from voting "by any means."

February 1946, Isaac Widar, a recently discharged black veteran still wearing his uniform, was blinded when police shoved their nightsticks into his eyes. In July, two black veterans and their wives were dragged from their automobile and shot.

President Truman could not stand by and let the situation deteriorate. The United States considered itself the leader of the free world. As former colonies in Asia and Africa won their independence, their people, most of them black or brown, were choosing between the capitalist system of the United States and Western Europe and the socialist system of the Soviet Union and Eastern Europe. A new "Cold War" was brewing between former allies—the Soviet Union and the United States. Soviet newspapers reported on "democratic" America's racial problem. On December 6, 1946, President Truman appointed the President's Committee on Civil Rights to study the racial problem. Civil rights fighters kept the pressure on throughout 1947, even appealing to the United Nations Human Rights Commission.

Because of the Cold War tensions, there were proposals to pass a law requiring all young men to receive military training. A. Philip Randolph and others organized the Committee Against Jim Crow in Military Service and Training, demanding full integration of the armed forces. The navy, still under Forrestal's command, had removed all racial restrictions from its regulations early in 1946, but the army, Air Corps and marines retained their World War II segregationist policies.

The report of the President's Committee on Civil

One of many wartime demonstrations
against Jim Crowism in the military

Rights, *To Secure These Rights*, was made public in May 1947. It stated that separate but equal was "one of the outstanding myths of the 20th century." A legislative program was recommended to bring civil rights to all Americans. Committee members agreed that military integration should be one of the first steps taken.

Most people believed that civil rights would again be blocked in Congress. President Truman was urged to issue an executive order, but he remained silent. Violence continued and segregation remained firmly in place.

Democrats feared that unless Truman acted he would lose the upcoming fall election. A. Philip Randolph once again decided that only a mass action would work. He urged black men to refuse to serve in a segregated army. Support for his proposal mounted.

The issue was pulling the Democratic party apart. At the Democratic National Convention, liberals narrowly passed a strong civil rights program. Many southern delegates stormed out of the hall and went home to form their own Dixiecrat party.

With southern support gone, President Truman had nothing left to lose. On July 26, 1948, he issued Executive Order 9981, calling for equality of opportunity for all persons in the armed services and creating the Committee on Equality of Treatment and Opportunity in the Armed Services to implement the order. Once again, there was no specific mention of integration.

Faced by disappointed civil rights advocates, President Truman quickly made a public statement that the intent of the order was integration. With a wait-and-see attitude, Randolph canceled his call for civil disobedience.

Black and white soldiers performing their
duties together in an integrated army
during the Korean War

In November, Harry S. Truman was elected by a narrow margin. But the army still ignored the president's executive order. Many believed that it would never be enforced. They did not reckon on the determination of A. Philip Randolph, the black veterans of World War II, and many other African-American men and women and their supporters. Nor did they correctly judge the tenacity of a tough man from Missouri named Harry S. Truman, who was determined to take this step.

During the Korean War in 1950, the last of the segregated units in the military disappeared. It had become obvious to all fair-minded observers that integration led to a decrease in racial conflict in the armed forces and an increase in efficiency.

In 1954, before the Supreme Court handed down its historic decision on school desegregation, some Court members studied a still unpublished manuscript on the struggle for military integration. It helped to convince the justices how evil and stupid segregation was.

In the 1990s, almost half a century since the end of World War II, for people of all races army life was often their first and only experience with interracial living. Despite the civil rights laws passed in the 1960s, Martin Luther King, Jr.'s dream of equality remained unfulfilled. Both housing and education remained largely segregated. Although some black Americans had moved into better jobs and professions, most were still locked in poverty, blocked by an invisible wall of prejudice.

The struggle for full equality for all people was far from over.

FOR FURTHER READING

Nonfiction

Fleming, Thomas J. *Give Me Liberty: Black Valor in the Revolutionary War*. New York: Scholastic, 1971.

Halliburton, Warren J. *The Fighting Red Tails: America's First Black Airmen*. New York: C.P.I. Publishing, Inc., 1978.

Henri, Florette. *Bitter Victory: A History of Black Soldiers in World War I*. Garden City, N.Y.: Doubleday, 1970.

Katz, William Loren. *World War II to the New Frontier, 1940–1963*. Austin, Tex.: Raintree Steck-Vaughn, 1993.

Mettger, Zak. *Till Victory Is Won: Black Soldiers in the Civil War*. New York: Lodestar Books, 1994.

Reef, Catherine. *Civil War Soldiers*. New York: Twenty-First Century Books, 1993.

Wright, David K. *A Multicultural Portrait of World War II*. New York: Marshall Cavendish, 1994.

Fiction

Clarke, John. *Black Soldier*. Garden City, N.Y.: Doubleday, 1968.

INDEX

ABOUT THE AUTHOR

Hedda Garza is a lecturer, an activist, and a prizewinning author. Among Garza's awards are *Choice* magazine's Outstanding Academic Book Award (1982) for the *Watergate Index*, and the New York Public Library's Best Book for Young Adults Award (1986).

355
GAR

Garza, Hedda.

Without regard to race

DATE DUE	BORROWER'S NAME	ROOM NUMBER